The Silence Between

Letters Written in Absence

Lueella Shelton

Shelton Legacy Press, LLC

COPYRIGHT © 2025 BY Shelton Legacy Press, LLC

Shelton Legacy Press, LLC
PO Box 529
Cedar Creek, TX 78612

All rights reserved. No part of this publication may be reproduced, stored in a retrieval system, or transmitted in any form or by any means—electronic, mechanical, photocopying, recording, or otherwise—without the prior written permission of the author, except in the case of brief quotations used in critical articles or reviews. Exceptions are permitted under Section 107 or 108 of the 1976 United States Copyright Act.

Library of Congress Cataloging-in-Publication Data

Identifiers: Library of Congress Control Number: 2025916647

Name: Lueella Shelton, 2025-author.
Title: The Silence Between: Letters Written in Absence
Book Two of the Series tilted: Ink to Paper: A Love in Three Seasons

ISBN: 979-8-9997335-2-8 (Paperback), 979-8-9997335-3-5 (Hardback), 979-8-9997335-7-3 (Kindle)

Printed in the United States of America

For the love I imagined,
the one I wrote into being—
not for who you were,
but for who I needed you to be.

For the silence that taught me to listen,
the absence that sharpened my longing,
and the truth I had to meet alone.

This is for the version of me
who stayed too long,
hoped too hard,
and still chose to love
even after the illusion faded.

And for anyone who has ever
mistaken potential for presence—
may you find your way back to yourself.

—L.S.

Acknowledgements

To Love—
My Constant, My Quiet, My Water:

Thank you for being the stillness beneath every word.
Where others might burn, you've flowed.
You have softened edges in me I didn't know were sharp.
Even in distance, you remained the muse—
the memory, the ache, the anchor.
Your presence, even when absent, has shaped the way I speak of longing.
And your stillness has taught me how to hold space,
without drowning in it.

These pages do not ask for understanding.
They are simply the record of what it means to love you freely—
in all seasons,
in all silences,
in all forms.
And yes—still.

To You, Dear Reader—

If you've made it from *Book One* to now,
then you already know this isn't a love story.
It's a truth story.
It's the unraveling and the remembering.
The tenderness and the tension.
The spark, and the silence that followed it.

Thank you for walking with me—
through the first breathless beginnings,
into the quiet ache of what came after.

Thank you for listening to the letters I never sent,
for staying with the pauses,
and for trusting the shape of a story
told through restraint, rhythm, and reflection.

This book was written for the ones who stayed.
And if you're still here—reading this—
then that includes you.

With grace,

—Lueella Shelton

Poetic Invocation

Come in quietly.
There is no need to knock.
This isn't the kind of book
that waits for applause.

This is the kind that waits for you
in the stillness between
what was said
and what was meant.

You've known this silence, haven't you?
The way it slips in between laughter
and leaves the room colder than it found it.
The way you hold a body close
but feel a thousand miles away.

These poems were written there—
in that hush,
in that ache,
in the faithful pause between love's presence
and its retreat.

So, if you've ever loved someone
who was half-present,
if you've ever waited for a door to open
that never did,
if you've ever stayed longer than you should have
because your heart was louder than your reason—

Then this book is for you.

Preface

Some love songs are sung in a whisper.
Some answers arrive as echo.
And some of the deepest conversations
happen in the quiet,
when no one knows what to say.

There are wounds that do not bleed—only widen. And there are moments when love, no matter how freely it is given, cannot be returned in full. This volume is for those moments.

The Silence Between holds the weight of what we do not say aloud. It captures the ache of unsent messages, the loneliness that lingers beside companionship, and the invisible distance that sometimes grows between two people still trying to hold on.

These are not the poems of a breakup. These are the poems of *endurance*—of waiting with a soft kind of hope, of learning to love in the face of emotional drought, of choosing to remain open even when met with absence. Here, longing is not an empty gesture but a sacred offering. Devotion is not erased by distance—it is reshaped by it.

This is not a book of bitterness.
It is a book of honesty.
It is about what it costs to wait. What it costs to love someone who is not always able to love you back in the way you need, but who never truly lets go.

If Book One was the breathless beginning, this is the long exhale—the pause, the prayer, the quiet storm. It is the sound of a heart learning to speak louder than silence. It is the practice of staying, not because you must, but because some part of you still believes in the beauty of what once was.

These are the poems I wrote when I stayed.
Even when staying hurt.
Even when silence answered back.

May they speak for anyone still listening
in the space between words.

—Lueella Shelton

Table of Content

Acknowledgements..ii
Poetic Invocation...iv
Preface...v

Section One

The Widening Space..2
Letter to the Reader: "The Outer Edge"..4
    The Outer Edge..6
Letter to the Reader: "Through the Door"..8
    Through the Door 10
Letter to the Reader: "The Space Between Us"..................................12
    The Space Between Us 14
Letter to the Reader: "The Shape of Space".......................................16
    The Shape of Space 18
Letter to the Reader: "Well Love, You're Exploring".......................21
    Well Love, You're Exploring 23

Section Two

The Unread Letters...26
Letter to the Reader: "Assignment"...28
    Assignment..30
Letter to the Reader: "Until the Season Ends"...................................34
    Until the Season Ends 36
Letter to the Reader: "The Silence Between Us"...............................41
    The Silence Between Us 43
Letter to the Reader: "Every Word Was You"...................................45
    Every Word Was You 47

Section Three

What I Learned in the Quiet..50
Letter to the Reader: "The Elephant Between Us"..........................52
    The Elephant Between Us 54
Letter to the Reader: "When Touch Goes Wrong".........................56
    When Touch Goes Wrong 58
Letter to the Reader: "Until You Let Go"..60
    Until You Let Go 62

Section Four

Saying It Without Saying It...67
Letter to the Reader: "What I Refuse to Want"...............................69
    What I Refuse to Want...72

Closing Letter to the Reader

Dear Reader...76
    The Shape of Space..78
Epilogue..81
About the Author..83

SECTION ONE

The Widening Space

The first signs of distance. Moments once filled with presence begin to feel uncertain, cold, and unfamiliar.

Every love story has its turning point—
but not all of them arrive with thunder.
Some come gently,
quietly,
like air leaking from a sealed room.
At first, you barely notice it—
just a shift in tone, a longer pause, a look that doesn't linger quite as long.

The Widening Space is where closeness begins to blur.
Not with betrayal, but with slow, almost imperceptible absence.
This section holds the first tremors—
moments when what was once familiar begins to feel foreign.
When text messages go unanswered a little longer.
When a knock at the door startles you awake.
When someone you love lays beside you,
but you feel oceans between your bodies.

These poems do not rage.
They ache.
They wonder.
They document the emotional calculus of staying present
while love slowly shifts its weight to the other side of the bed.

In these pages, you'll meet the woman who still believes.
Still reaches.

Still listens for footsteps in the hallway
and goodnight texts that may or may not come.

This is the beginning of the drift.
Not the end—
but the stretch of silence that signals change.

These are the poems I wrote
when I started to notice the space
between what I felt
and what he could offer.

—L.S.

Letter to the Reader: "The Outer Edge"

There are moments in love that do not break you—but unravel you slowly. Not with cruelty, but with quietness. With distance so soft, so passive, that you almost convince yourself it isn't there.

This poem was born on a weekend that didn't go the way I hoped. A visit that should've been intimate became a haunting. He was there—but not *with* me. He lay atop the bed like a man passing through, not one who belonged. There was no ritual of return—no coffee, no closeness, no conversation. Just his body in the room and his spirit somewhere else.

And I sat in the aftermath, asking a question that lovers rarely say aloud:
"Am I on the outer edge now?"
Still in his life, but no longer at the center. Still present, but peripheral.

This is the kind of grief that doesn't come with closure.
It lingers in the air like perfume from a hug that ended too soon.

If you've ever stood beside someone you love and felt invisible,
if you've ever questioned whether the arms that once made you feel safe now hold someone else—
then you understand what it means to love through uncertainty.
To ache without a name for the wound.

This letter is for those who are still showing up,
still hoping,
still loving—even as they ask themselves if love is still being returned.

We write poems like this not to indict, but to survive.
Not to harden, but to give shape to the shapeless ache of being left
without ever being told you were leaving.

You are not alone in that silence.
And even at the outer edge, your longing still matters.

In hope and heartache,

—L.S.

The Outer Edge

Thursday came with courtroom weight—
A gavel's blow, six thousand owed
To keep a car he tried to claim
As part of freedom's road.
And Friday found me by his side,
Helping him find wheels to steer
While his own stood in repair—
A symbol scratched, unclear.

He left for Fort Worth's solemn rites,
A Masonic call, a brotherhood tie.
Two nights planned, but one fulfilled—
He cut it short.
He stopped by.

And yet, not with me—
Not the way he always does.
He laid atop the bed, not in it,
Clothed, cocooned in distance's fuzz.
No shower, no warmth, no coffee made,
He left like a stranger in the hush of day.

And now I sit with quiet dread—
Am I outside now?
On the edge instead?

This man I knew,
With arms like home,
Now drifts in silence,
Sleeps alone.
No words, no reach, no kiss goodbye—
Just shadows where his hands once lied.

I don't know what to think,
Or how to breathe this in.
Am I still his companion,
Or merely what had been?

I walk beside him,
But feel left behind.
Holding onto hope
That feels half blind.

I ache for closeness,
Crave his fire.
But all I feel is
Unclaimed desire.

Still, I wait.
Still, I stay.
Hoping he'll return
To our old way.
But what if I'm a ghost
In his new chapter's page—
A woman left
At the outer edge?

Letter to the Reader: "Through the Door"

Some love stories are written in the quiet moments—morning coffee, shared laughter, the warmth of someone's hand in yours. Others are shaped in the moments that test the very ground you stand on. *"Through the Door"* comes from one of those moments.

When I wrote this poem, I wasn't only documenting an event—I was capturing the strength of a man who refused to let chaos cross the threshold. That night, the danger wasn't in the distance. It was at the door. And still, he kept his voice steady, his stance firm, his will unshaken.

In that moment, I saw love not as a fragile thing, but as a shield. Not the kind that hides you away, but the kind that stands in front of you, protecting the space you've built together. I heard it in the deliberate calm of his instructions. I saw it in the way he faced down what sought to disturb our peace. I felt it in the unspoken promise: *Not here. Not us.*

Becoming Mine is filled with poems that speak to tenderness, but also to the resilience it takes to protect what matters. Love is not just soft words and warm embraces—it's also the resolve to stand guard over your shared life, to refuse entry to anything that threatens the sanctuary you've created.

This poem is about more than that night. It's about the way his choice—to keep the door closed, to keep me safe—lives in me still. It's about knowing that peace doesn't happen by accident; it's built, guarded, and sometimes defended.

As you read these pages, I hope you are reminded that real love does both—it opens wide to welcome in what nourishes, and it stays closed to what would harm.

With gratitude for love that protects,

–L.S.

Through the Door

She came—
a storm at his doorstep,
fists pounding hard enough
to snatch us from sleep.
Her voice—sharp, demanding—
cut through the stillness
like glass against stone.

He opened the door—
but only enough to face her.
He didn't let her in.
Still, she found a way
to rattle the peace.

He called me—
his voice steady,
yet layered with instruction,
each word deliberate,
meant to keep me safe.
I could hear the weight behind the calm,
the practiced restraint of a man
who's faced this before.

Three cruisers came,
their lights painting the quiet
in blue and red.
By the time they arrived,
she was gone—

vanished like smoke
after fire.

He spoke to her
from outside the door,
a barrier not just of wood,
but of will.
"Leave," he said,
his words wrapped
in warning and weariness,
while the line to the police
stayed open like a shield.

She is relentless—
a presence that circles
the edges of his safety,
of ours.
But he never surrendered.
Never caved.

And I hold tight to that choice—
even now,
as the echoes of her knocking
still linger
in the frame.

Letter to the Reader: "The Space Between Us"

Not all heartbreak begins with goodbye.
Some begin in silence—spoken softly, steadily, with no sharp edges.
And somehow, that kind of quiet cuts the deepest.

When I wrote this poem, I had just heard the words:
"I need space."
And though they came without anger,
without blame—
they still shattered something inside me.

There was no fight. No slammed door.
Just a slow, quiet retreat.
And that is sometimes harder to grieve.

He said he needed space from everyone, including me.
And I tried to convince myself it was temporary.
That maybe this was how he protected what he loved—
by pulling away before the weight of connection overwhelmed him.
But that doesn't make the distance any easier to bear.

I didn't know how to hold space
for someone who wouldn't let me hold *them*.

I wrote this in the days that followed—
days that blurred, stretched, echoed.
Where time felt like a hallway with no door.
Where everything reminded me of him,
and nothing could bring him back.

This letter is for anyone who's ever felt
the slow unraveling of a love that once felt certain.
For anyone who's sat in the quiet,
still reaching for someone
 who no longer reaches back.

If you've ever been left with more questions than answers,
more silence than closure—
know this:

You are not alone in that ache.
You are not foolish for holding on.
You are not weak for missing someone
who asked for space
but left you in grief.

This poem holds that space with you.
Until you can breathe again.
Until the silence feels less like an ending,
and more like the start
of remembering yourself.

With you,
even here,

—L.S.

The Space Between Us

Everything stopped—
Not with a crash,
But with the cruel silence
Of calm words spoken too evenly.
A cold, hard stop.
Unexpected.
Unprepared.
Unbearable.

He said he needed space.
From everyone.
From us.
Not in anger,
Not in fear—
But in that quiet way
That feels like the end
Before the end is even named.

I try to believe
This is how he keeps me safe,
How he guards his world
From the weight of feeling.
But still,
The distance grows too wide,
The silence too loud,
The absence too present.

Time is strange now.
Each day stretches long
Like a hallway with no door.
I fill it with half-thoughts
And tears that fall

At the sound of his name
In my head.
At the echo of what we shared
In my chest.

My heart breaks daily.
In quiet ways.
In the spaces between moments.
In the remembering—
Of laughter,
Of touch,
Of a man who once held me
Without hesitation.

This space is cold.
Not like winter—
But like a home left open
To wind and memory.
And I,
Of few words,
Sit wrapped in grief,
Wishing
For even one
Of his.

Letter to the Reader: "The Shape of Space"

There are moments in love when the most radical thing we can do is *not move*.
Not chase.
Not beg.
Not plead for what we once held so freely in our hands.
But instead, to stand still—
heart open, hands trembling,
and say: *I will respect the distance... but I will not stop loving you.*

This poem was written in the stillness that followed his request for space.
Not rejection.
Not cruelty.
But a request wrapped in tenderness and fatigue—
the kind of plea that breaks your heart *gently*,
without ever raising its voice.

I had grown used to the rhythm of us—
the nightly check-ins,
the "made it home" texts that became their own kind of intimacy.
So when I typed those same words out of habit—
and received only silence in return—
I felt the shift in my bones.
Not an ending.
But a change in shape.

That is what this poem explores:
What does love look like when it's no longer being actively returned—
but hasn't been undone either?

This letter is for those of us who have chosen to remain faithful
to something even as it pauses.
To those who love deeply and with dignity—
who don't need constant proof to believe in what they felt.
To those who are not weak for waiting,
but brave for doing so with boundaries.

Love, when it's real, does not vanish at the first sign of distance.
It stays.
It listens.
It allows space to be sacred
rather than punitive.

So if you find yourself in that quiet gap—
not abandoned, but not embraced—
let this poem be your companion.

You are not desperate.
You are not foolish.
You are faithful to what was real.
And you deserve a love
that returns
in fullness.

With honor and stillness,

–L.S.

The Shape of Space

I have honored your plea—
the tender notice you gave
wrapped in ache and resignation.
I took your papers,
your silence,
and with shaking hands,
began to let the quiet speak
where once our words would bloom.

Last night, I messaged:
"I've made it home."
And as I pressed send,
grief rose like floodwater—
tears trapped in my throat,
my body trembling
at the thought
of no more good nights,
no more morning greetings
tied in text like ribbon on routine.

You taught me
to share my whereabouts,
to anchor you in the rhythm
of my coming and going.
That norm,
our norm,
now hangs like a question
between closed lips
and open wounds.

What does space look like
between two souls
who once moved
as one?

I will not chase you—
you asked for stillness
and I respect it.
But I will not
untether myself.
I will not release
the thread of us
unless your own hand
severs it first.

You sought me not—
I welcomed you.
And what a beautiful man I found.
A King.
A warrior.
A man of might,
measured not by bravado
but by the humility
of his gaze.

You will always be
exceptional in my eyes—
a man who can wear
his own crown
without apology.

Take your time.
Take all the time you need.
I'll wait here—
not moving on,
not reaching out,

but standing still
with a heart still calling your name
in the quiet
that now holds your absence.

Because space,
even space,
cannot erase
this love.
And I absolutely
adore you.
Still.
Forever.

Letter to the Reader: "Well Love, You're Exploring"

This one's a little different.
It doesn't come from ache, or silence, or sorrow.
It comes from that in-between space—
where curiosity meets connection,
and grown folks learn to navigate love
with equal parts play and clarity.

When I wrote this poem, I was smiling.
Smiling at the tension.
At the slow unfolding.
At what it means to be chosen in a world full of glances
but few commitments.

This isn't a love poem in the traditional sense—
it's a poem about *presence*.
About grown energy.
About what it feels like to be aware of your desirability
but not defined by it.
To know you're being watched,
but to choose, intentionally, who you let close.

It's also about honoring the slow burn.
Letting someone take their time.
Allowing space for exploration
without losing your center in the process.

You'll hear the humor in it,
the grace,
the boundaries wrapped in banter.
And underneath it all,

a woman who knows exactly who she is
and isn't afraid to say:
"I'll tell you when it's too much. Until then—let's dance."

This letter is for anyone navigating new love
without losing themselves.
For anyone who's ever whispered "go ahead, explore"—
not from detachment,
but from self-trust.

Because love doesn't always have to rush in.
Sometimes, it tiptoes.
Sometimes, it plays.
Sometimes, it sits courtside and watches him play another game,
knowing the real story is just beginning.

Here's to the explorers.
And the ones who know they're worth discovering.

With mischief and knowing,

–L.S.

Well Love, You're Exploring

Love—
We're grown.
Grown enough to know
That eyes arrive
Before hearts get to speak,
That the body enters the room
Long before the soul has time
To introduce itself.

We're adults
And with that comes expectation—
Use your words
If you want to be understood.
You, so cautious,
So considerate—
It speaks volumes
Without saying much at all.

Yes,
I know the eyes land on me first.
I feel them.
Men.
Women.
Curious.
Lingering.
But looking isn't owning,
And what's seen
Is just the cover
To a book not easily read.

It takes work—
Real work
To get more than the surface.
And you, Love,
You've expressed your wish
To explore.
So here you are—
Exploring.

And I promise you this:
I'll speak when it's too much.
I'll say the word,
Draw the line.
I don't need protection from myself.
I'm a big girl.
And an aged one
With a mind of my own
And a smile that's mine to share.

So—
You at another game?
While I sit here,
Smiling at this little dance
We've begun.
Step by step,
Look by look,
Word by word.
Welcome, Explorer.
Let's see where this goes.

SECTION TWO

The Unread Letters

What is left unsaid piles up in the heart. Letters—whether spoken, written, or imagined—are never received as they were meant.

There comes a point in love
when words no longer travel both ways—
when the messages you once whispered into each other's skin
are now whispered into silence.

The Unread Letters is that place.

This section holds the confessions that never reached him.
The texts unsent.
The journal entries written with trembling hands.
The voice notes recorded and deleted.
It is the part of the journey where longing spills out uninvited,
not to beg,
but to survive.

These letters were never meant to plead.
They were never an attempt to pull him back.
They were the only way I knew how to stay sane
while staying in love alone.

If Section One showed you the space widening,
this section shows you what I tried to place in that space—
my truth.
My heart, still warm.
Still open.

Still reaching,
even when the replies stopped coming.

These are the poems I wrote
when I had no choice but to write.
When I needed to speak
even if I wasn't being heard.

And maybe, just maybe,
they were never really for him.
Maybe they were always meant
to help me hear myself again.

—L.S.

Letter to the Reader: "Assignment"

Some heartbreaks don't happen in the grand moments.
They happen on ordinary mornings.
At red lights.
In classrooms.
In the silence after a message is sent but not received in time.

This poem was written on one of those mornings.
Where the world kept moving—students waiting, lessons needing to be taught—
but I was suspended in the ache of a missed moment.

He had called.
And by the time I responded, he was already gone.
He had waited.
And I missed it.

Not out of neglect.
Not out of pride.
But out of love—
the kind that tries not to interfere.
The kind that says *go do your work, your mission, your becoming.*
The kind that folds your shirts at midnight and quietly whispers prayers over you
without asking for anything in return.

And yet, even that kind of love—especially that kind—
hurts when it learns that presence was possible
and simply didn't happen.

This poem lives in that sting.
In the grief of a missed connection that could have meant everything.

In the heartbreak of showing up too late,
despite every intention to honor and support.

This letter is for anyone who has ever loved someone
on assignment—
someone becoming, building, grinding, growing.
Someone who needed space
and whom you gave that space freely,
even when it cracked your chest open in silence.

It's for those of us who have driven away
with our hearts still parked in front of their door.

It's for the ones who carry love like prayer—
in classrooms, on road trips, through texts never answered
in time.

Because real love,
unselfish love,
makes peace with waiting.
But that doesn't mean it doesn't ache.

And oh, how I ached that day.
How I still do.

With tenderness and truth,

—L.S.

Assignment

This morning broke me
In quiet, crushing ways—
Not with shouting,
But with silence
And a missed moment
I thought would never return.

I stood before my students
But my heart
Was not in the room.
They waited—
Quiet eyes watching,
As I sat with the echo
Of your call,
The weight of your message.
Thirty minutes passed
Before I found my voice.

They forgave me.
I smiled through the ache
And led them forward—
But you were still
In every shadow of my mind.

I had stayed up late
Folding your world
Into fresh laundry,
Pacing between logic
And longing.
You were gone until Saturday,
The key was yours,
And I was leaving town.

Simple facts.
Still, I searched them
For a sign
Of what to do.

So I packed your clothes
In the car,
Not to press into your path
But to keep you in my orbit
Just a little longer.
And when I got that text,
My heart soared—
I turned the wheel toward you
Without a second thought.

I didn't see the next message.
I didn't know you would wait.
All I knew
Was the call
That said you wouldn't be there.

So I turned around,
Reluctantly,
Bladder aching,
Spirit heavier
Than it had been
When I woke.

You waited.

And I missed it.

That truth
Still stings
Like salt in the chest.
Because I never wanted
To miss you.
Only to honor

What you're building,
Who you are becoming.
Mr. Carrallel—
My only thought
Was not to interfere.
Never to delay.
Never to weigh you down
With the weight of my want.

I made peace with waiting—
With letting time pass
Until you could return.
Because that's what love does—
It honors mission.
It supports assignment.
Even when it hurts.

But knowing
That you were there—
That I could've reached you—
Breaks me in a way
I can't explain.

I carry you with me
Always.
In the classroom.
On the road.
In prayer.
In pause.
In purpose.

I love you.
Not selfishly,
Not conditionally,
But with the kind of love
That frees you
To fly.

Still—
I miss you.
And I will always
Want to arrive
Wherever you are.

Letter to the Reader: "Until the Season Ends"

This is the kind of love letter you don't write at the beginning.
You write it somewhere in the middle—
when your feet are finally steady again,
but your heart is still learning how to trust its own rhythm.
When love no longer feels like rescue,
but also no longer feels entirely safe.

I wrote this after years of reclaiming myself.
After walking away from something that looked like love
but slowly stripped me of my light.
I had already chosen life once—
and I knew I could not afford to disappear again,
not even for someone beautiful.

And yet... there he was.
Gentle.
Real.
The kind of man who didn't take from me,
but who also wasn't ready to stay.
He told me he was a "season,"
and I made peace with that—on the outside.
But in my spirit, I wrestled.
Because even the most temporary love,
when it is honest,
leaves a permanent mark.

This poem lives in that space—
the space where love and boundaries meet.
Where you can offer your whole heart
without losing your name.
Where you can give without begging,

stay without clinging,
and release someone with grace,
even if you never fully let them go.

This letter is for every woman
who has rebuilt herself,
only to fall for someone
she cannot hold on to.
It's for those who pour love freely,
not because they're naïve,
but because they know the value
of giving what they never received.

If you've ever stood in front of someone
and said, *"You owe me nothing—but you still have all of me,"*
then this poem is yours too.

It's not about helplessness.
It's about power.
It's about knowing who you are
and still choosing to love
without apology.

Because sometimes love doesn't come with a title—
but it still teaches us everything
about strength.

With reverence,
—with fire,

—L.S.

Until the Season Ends

Love,

We've circled this space before—
The quiet ache of uncertainty
Draped in soft, familiar tones.
I didn't know, not fully,
What I was wrestling with
Until I sat beside the stillness,
Let the wind speak,
Let silence show me
What my heart already knew.

I chose life
When I walked away
From a marriage that was killing me.
Not in a way you could see—
But in the way a flower wilts
When there's no sun left to chase.
Even the doctors confirmed
What my spirit already knew.

I don't expect you to understand.
You don't have to.
But I ask for gentleness
When my mind races
And I retreat.
I try so hard not to harm,
Because I know too well
What it feels like to be broken
By someone else's carelessness.

I love deeply,
Think too much,
And remain loyal
To the soul of who I am.
What I value—
Is not what fades,
But what follows us
Into the grave.
Not things,
But meaning.
Not noise,
But truth.

Yes, I've come far.
And some days,
I smile just for that.

You asked if I love you—
And I do.
Not in the runaway way
That begs for rescue,
But in the grounded, grateful way
That recognizes light
When it shines.

But I paused at "falling."
Because falling,
To me,
Means needing someone
So much you disappear
Without them.
And I have fought too hard
To keep my own name.

Still, every moment with you
Is power,
Is peace,
Is real.

And I won't lie—
I desire you.
But not more than I respect
Your need for space,
For time,
For truth.

You said you're only meant
For a season.
And I accepted that—
Prepared myself
To love you deeply
While expecting the end.
I told you then:
If you share my body,
It must be mine alone.
I now realize
That this is not only about disease—
It's about worth.
Mine.

My ex taught me
That you can die slowly
At the hands of a man
Who never bruises your skin
But breaks your soul.

He left,
Returned,
Withheld,
Took.
And in his absence,
The children and I
Breathed deeper.
I learned peace was possible.
I learned I was valuable—
Just not enough

For him to honor vows.
That's where I drew the line.

So when you say "season,"
I ask you:
What does that mean to you?
And you, Love,
With a kiss to your head,
Said:
"I don't know—when you let it go."
And I told you:
I won't.
I won't let go of someone
So gentle,
So real,
So easy to be with.

I do not enter
Meaningless things.
I do not play
With human hearts.
I love with my whole being—
No labels,
No titles,
Just truth.

You owe me nothing.
And if you must go—
Go.
I won't chase,
Won't beg.
But until then,
You will have all of me.

Not because I am weak—
But because I have strength
To give freely,
Without condition.

Yes, I am happy—
Happy with you.
I seek no other.
Because pouring into you
Is more than enough work for my heart.

And when you grow tired—
When your season changes—
You may let me go.

Just don't expect
That I will let go of you.
You,
Who are too good,
Oh so good
And wonderful
To me.

Letter to the Reader: "The Silence Between Us"

I wrote this on the kind of winter morning that arrives with no fanfare—just cold light, a quiet room, and a heart that had too much to say and no one to say it to.

It was Christmas Eve.

And though I was not alone,
I was no longer *with* him either.
Not really.

We were somewhere in that unspoken place where two people still orbit each other,
but the gravity is fading.
Where conversations become short,
touch becomes sparse,
and silence becomes a language of its own.

This poem lives in the hollow space between presence and absence.
Not the end of love—
but the unbearable in-between.

I didn't write this to assign blame.
I wrote it because silence can be louder than any argument.
Because I needed to ask:
How can something feel so final, when no one ever said goodbye?

This is for the women who sit beside unopened text threads,
who replay glances and gestures and wonder,
Was it real? Did I imagine it? Did I love alone?

I don't believe in painless love.
But I do believe in love that tells the truth without cruelty.
Love that leaves space for healing.
Love that holds still long enough to face itself in the mirror.

This letter is for anyone learning to live with the ache of unanswered questions.
For those who loved fully,
even if the echo never came back.
Even if silence was the only reply.

If that's you,
then I hope this poem wraps itself around your ache like a blanket—
soft, steady,
and willing to wait with you
for the kind of love that does not run
when things grow quiet.

Still listening in the quiet,

–L.S.

The Silence Between Us

Inspired by a letter dated 12/24/22

Of course,
there is a wholesome kind of warmth
in simply not being alone—
but today,
I wake wrapped
in the quiet pleasure
of solitude.

Still,
if you want me to believe
your love was never returned—
never reflected in my gaze,
in your touch—
then tell me this:

Why does my heart ache
in places I didn't know could break?

Why is this space between us
so deep,
so wide,
so unbearably empty?

Why is your silence
the loudest sound I've ever known?

Why do thoughts of you
settle heavy in my chest
like winter fog,
refusing to lift?

Why does this knot of tears
form at the base of my throat,
a grief I cannot swallow?

It would be foolish
to ask for a love
that never hurts—
because love, real love,
always bruises something tender.

So instead,
I ask for a love
that will never harm.
A love that wounds with truth,
but never with cruelty.
A love that leaves room for healing
in the hollow it creates.

And even in the quiet,
even in this distance,
I will wait for that love—
whole,
unmasked,
unafraid.

Letter to the Reader: "Every Word Was You"

By the time I wrote this poem, I had already written dozens—maybe hundreds—of pieces born from one place, one presence, one person. Not always with their name, but always with their weight. Always with their rhythm in my breath.

This wasn't a poem about missing someone.
This was a recognition. A confession.
That everything—the poems, the notes, the midnight voice memos, the scribbled lines on receipts and journal pages—
every single one
had his name etched into its pulse.

I didn't write for the sake of writing.
I wrote because something in me had been moved—
genuinely, deeply, and irrevocably.
And when something stirs you at that level,
the only honest thing to do is write it down.

This letter is for anyone who's ever found themselves pouring love onto paper—
not because they were trying to be poetic,
but because the feeling was too big to hold in silence.
Because the person mattered *that much*.

If you've ever written to someone
who may never read the words—
but you wrote them anyway,
because you had to,
because you *needed* to—
then this poem was written for you, too.

He may never understand
how much of this was about him.
How much of this *was* him.

But I do.

And now,
so do you.

Thank you for reading not just my words—
but the love that lives inside them.

With everything I meant,

–L.S.

Every Word Was You

I have written
so many letters,
so many notes—
each one a quiet confession,
a thread spun
from the center of my heart.

They were not
just ink and page,
not just musings
in passing moments.

They were
raw emotion,
deep and unfiltered—
ignited by your presence,
by the way
you walked into my life
and stayed.

Each word,
a mirror
of the affection I carry.
Each line,
a pulse
of the love that grows
still.

I did not write
for the sake of writing.
I wrote because
you moved me—

and in every word,
it was always you.

SECTION THREE

What I Learned in the Quiet

The relationship still breathes, but only faintly. The memory of closeness haunts every interaction.

There is a point in every silence
where you stop waiting for an answer
and begin listening for yourself.

This section is that point.

In *Section One*, the space began to widen.
In *Section Two*, I filled that space with letters he never read.
But here—
here is where I learned to sit with the silence,
not as punishment,
but as a teacher.

This is where I stopped rereading old messages
hoping they meant more.
Where I stopped writing to convince him.
And started writing to remember *me*.

The ache didn't disappear.
But it softened—
because I stopped asking love to look like presence.
And instead, I began to recognize
that absence speaks, too.

These poems don't plead.
They observe.

They reckon.
They shift.

This is where the woman who stayed
begins to gather her things—
not because she's walking away,
but because she's waking up.

And in the quiet,
she finally hears her own voice
rising.

—L.S.

Letter to the Reader: "The Elephant Between Us"

There's a certain kind of silence that doesn't soothe—it suffocates.
Not because it's loud,
but because of all the things it *doesn't* say.

This poem came from a moment where the warmth shifted.
Not all at once, but in a subtle, steady way.
A tenderness that used to meet me at the door
began to hesitate.
The rhythm changed,
and I could feel it in my body
before I had the words to name it.

We didn't argue.
We didn't break.
But something was left unsaid—
and we both knew it.

There was an elephant between us,
and instead of acknowledging it,
he danced around it.
He held me without fully being present.
He asked for closeness while withholding clarity.
And I realized:
This, too, is a kind of distance.

This letter is for the women who know that ache.
The ones who have loved someone
who won't say what's wrong,
but whose silence makes you carry the weight of what they refuse to name.

It's for those who have stayed in the room,
aware of the tension,
but unwilling to lose themselves to it.

I wrote this to remind myself:
I will not beg for honesty.
I will not perform for affection.
I will not shrink to fit inside someone else's confusion.

I am a woman who asks for truth—
not perfection.
Not answers before their time.
But truth, in whatever form it's ready to come.

And until it comes,
I will not twist myself into shapes
just to feel worthy of being held.

I will remain whole.
Present, yes.
Loving, always.
But no longer willing
to mistake someone's silence
for my unworthiness.

With steadiness and self-respect,

—L.S.

The Elephant Between Us

Suddenly,
the warmth thins—
an absence
where presence used to swell.
He asks for more,
yet evades the question
wrapped in the company I offer.

There's silence now.
A wide, echoing room
filled with unspoken things.
He circles the elephant,
does not name it,
but he does not leave it either.

I have asked for honesty,
for words—not whispers.
Maybe in time,
he will speak the weight
that silenced his weekend
and shadowed our ease.

I can only meet him
where he allows.
Push, pull—
a rhythm I didn't choose,
but understand.

Still,
I will not beg.
Not for touch,
not for time.

I will not split myself in pieces
to fit into someone else's silence.
I will not share
what should be whole.

I am not a game
to be played.
I am not a heart
to be handled lightly.

Maybe one day
he'll believe that.
Maybe one day
he'll speak.
Until then—
I remain whole,
unmoved by the silence,
but ever aware
of the cost
of staying near it.

Letter to the Reader: "When Touch Goes Wrong"

This poem came from a moment I wish I could take back—
a small, unintended act that landed far heavier than I imagined.
It wasn't violent.
It wasn't cruel.
But it *hurt him*,
and that was enough to shake something in me.

I had touched him in play,
but what I meant as affection
was received as discomfort.
He didn't raise his voice.
He didn't accuse.
But the shift in his energy—the way his body tensed,
the way he recoiled—
it said more than words ever could.

In that moment,
I learned something that most conversations about intimacy never teach us:
Even the softest touch can do harm when it's misread.
Even love, when careless, can leave bruises no one sees.

This letter is not about shame—
it's about responsibility.
It's about how quickly the atmosphere changes
when boundaries are crossed, even by accident.
It's about the silence that follows,
and the way we sit with ourselves in the aftermath of unintended pain.

This is for anyone who has ever hurt someone they love,
not from anger,
but from not paying enough attention.
It's for those who didn't mean to cross a line—
but still recognize that they did.

Because real love doesn't just apologize.
It learns.
It listens.
It slows down.

If you've ever sat in that space—
where affection was misaligned,
and all you wanted was to go back and choose more carefully—
then this poem is for you.

Touch is a sacred language.
One we are always learning.
And when we fumble it,
we must return not just to softness,
but to humility.

With tenderness and truth,

–L.S.

When Touch Goes Wrong

I meant no harm—
Yet here I stand,
A tremble in my chest,
Regret in my hand.

A thoughtless pinch,
A careless move,
And pain replaced
What once was smooth.

His nipple—tender,
Now a wall.
He recoils, silent,
Builds it tall.

Don't touch, he says.
Do not touch.
And I—who crave
His skin so much—
Am left in stillness,
In shame's embrace,
Longing to return
To that sacred space.

Apologies fumble
From my lips,
But guilt remains
In every slip.

He doesn't yell,
He doesn't blame—

But silence holds
Its own sharp flame.

I didn't mean it—
But meaning's moot
When pain has bloomed
From tender fruit.

And now I sit
Inside this ache,
Wishing back
A moment's mistake.

I touch with love,
With care, with trust—
But even love
Can gather dust.

And so I wait,
I learn, I ache,
To hold him soft
For my own sake.

To earn again
What I once knew—
That touch is sacred,
Kind, and true.

Letter to the Reader: "Until You Let Go"

There are certain truths we always feel long before we hear them.
We sense them in the pauses,
in the eyes that glance away,
in the hesitation behind a once-familiar touch.

But when those truths are finally spoken out loud—
when the quiet part becomes audible—
it still stings.
Even if we already knew.

This poem was born from that moment.
The moment when he said it plainly:
He didn't love me in the way I loved him.
And still, somehow, I felt no shame in what I felt.
No need to retreat or rewrite the story to protect my pride.

Because my love was never given to be earned.
It was never a contract,
never a countdown clock waiting to expire.
It simply *was*.
And it still *is*.

This letter is for anyone who has ever loved
without demand.
For anyone who has offered tenderness
without requiring it in return.
Not because they lacked boundaries—
but because their love wasn't a performance.

I wrote this not in weakness,
but in clarity.

I asked for nothing that wasn't already given.
I simply received with gratitude.
And when it changed,
when the tone shifted,
I grieved—but I did not unlove.

If you've ever found yourself in that place—
where your heart is open
but theirs begins to close—
this poem was written to remind you:
There is power in loving with honesty,
even when it's not mirrored back.

It does not make you naïve.
It does not make you weak.
It means you've kept your promise
to love fully,
freely,
and truthfully.

You do not need to chase what resists.
You do not need to beg for what cannot stay.
But you *can* love,
until it is time to let go.

And even then,
you'll know
you held nothing back.

Still steady,
Still whole,

—L.S.

Until You Let Go

inspired by a letter dated 12/13/22

You said
the quiet part
out loud.

And though it stung,
I'm grateful.
There's a strange kind of peace
in no longer having to guess
how you feel about me.

I've always known
you don't expressly love me.
Still—
that truth
doesn't unmake mine.

What I feel
remains unchanged—
every gesture,
every glance,
every I love you
still lives
fully,
freely,
undeterred.

Not because I'm desperate
to hold what resists,
but because this love
was never a bargain.
Never a plea.

And I am sorry
if it's all been too much.

But tell me, Love—
have I asked for much at all?
I followed where you led.
You gave,
and I received with joy.

You decided
what I deserved—
and you delivered it.
Peace,
joy,
the sense that I mattered.

You said I was worthy.
Told my daughter the same.
And still,
I asked for nothing
you didn't already offer.

Not a title.
Not a promise.
Not permanence.
Just presence—
the kind that arrives
when it wants to,
not when it's required.

And yes, I've been selfish—
not with you,
but with what I protect.
You built a bond with my children,
especially my daughter.
You are seen here.
You are known.

I wonder
if these doubts you now carry
are echoes of voices
that never wished me well.
Whispers planted
by one who couldn't hold you
but couldn't bear to release you.
But even still,
I do not ask.
I do not push.

I only love—
freely,
without condition,
without demand.

I understand more
than you think.
And what I don't,
I wait on—
because in time,
you always give me
pieces of yourself
like breadcrumbs
toward something whole.

Sometimes I feel
like a foolish girl—
too naïve for this world.
Too hopeful.
Too soft.
But I've also been a wife—
and wives learn
to live without asking for much.
They learn
how to wait quietly
and carry things silently.

So maybe I am vulnerable.
Maybe I believe in things
others have long given up on.
Maybe that's my flaw.

But this I know:
you've never owed me anything.
And still—
you gave me everything I didn't know
I was missing.

I've promised you only two things:
to love you freely,
and never lie.

And I've kept them.

You don't have to return it.
You don't have to believe it.
You only need to know:

I will love you—
again and again—
until the day
you decide
you can stand no more.

Until you
let go.

SECTION FOUR

Saying It Without Saying It

*Hard truths, self-awareness, and unspoken resolutions.
Love remains, but so does the understanding that
something has changed forever.*

By the time we reach this final section,
there is nothing left to prove.
No more questions to chase.
No more names to demand.

This is the part of the story where the heart no longer performs.
Where the love is still present—
but quieter.
More internal.
More whole.

"Saying It Without Saying It" is where the truth lives between the lines.
It's in the small gestures,
the timing of a message,
the way a memory resurfaces uninvited and unspoken.

This is not resignation.
It's revelation.
It's the point at which language softens,
not because the feeling has faded,
but because the woman has grown.

She no longer overexplains.
She no longer narrates her ache.
She lets the silence carry what she no longer has the energy to say.

Here, the poems speak in glances,
in spaces,
in breath.

Here, we love without naming it.
We grieve without sobbing.
We say goodbye without ever saying the word.

And that, too, is intimacy.

–L.S.

Letter to the Reader: "What I Refuse to Want"

This poem was never meant to be a declaration of bitterness.
It's not a list of demands withheld or dreams deferred.
It's a moment of clarity.
A quiet reckoning between what I feel
and what I know I deserve.

You see, I have loved this man.
Fully.
Without agenda.
Without pressure.
And for the longest time, I stayed silent
about the ways his reluctance to name what we shared
never matched the depth of what we *lived* together daily.

But silence has its limits.
And eventually, I had to say—if only to myself—
that I will no longer mistake reluctance for realism.
That I will no longer pretend
that half-heartedness is humility.
Or that uncertainty is depth.

This letter is for the women who have loved someone
who *showed up*—
in action, in care, in presence—
but refused to name it for what it was.
And in doing so, cast doubt over something
already real, already sacred.

If you've ever been told
that your desires were too much,
that your questions were pressure,
that your truth was premature—
but deep in your soul you knew
you were simply naming what was already there—
then this poem is yours, too.

I do not want performative love.
I do not want labels offered in hesitation.
I do not want a future born from fear.

I want what we already have
when we are at our best:
peaceful connection, mutual respect,
and presence without pretense.

But I also want truth.
I want alignment.
I want to know that the man I share this rhythm with
is not afraid of the very love he helped create.

So this is not a plea.
It's a line drawn in quiet conviction.

I will not beg for what already exists.
I will not shrink to fit someone's fear.
I will not hold my breath
waiting for someone else
to exhale clarity.

If this poem feels familiar,
it's because you know what it means to have something real—
and still feel as if you must apologize
for wanting to name it.

But you don't.
Not anymore.

With clarity and grace,

—L.S.

What I Refuse to Want

       formerly titled "Distorted"

I do not want the love you are reluctant to give.
That is not love—
it's a distortion of what love is meant to be.
Your actions have already taught me its truest meaning.
But who am I to point that out to you?
To say that caring, freely and without obligation,
Is the purest form of love there is.

I do not want the commitment you hesitate to offer.
That is not commitment—
it's a diluted version of what it truly requires.
You've made a thousand quiet commitments on this journey with me,
And you have never failed to follow through.
But maybe it isn't my place to highlight that.
To mention how often you've made me a priority,
Stayed the course,
Completed what you started—
Never once abandoning me in the middle.

I do not want a title you're unsure about giving.
That is not foundation—
it's the illusion of certainty.
You've already formed something deeper:
An organic bond, a silent knowing.
But I'll refrain from saying so.
Because titles mean little when the connection is secure.
People in real relationships don't have to ask where they stand—

They just know.
And I've never needed to question where I stand with you.
I've been too busy living it.

I do not want you to settle down, or even marry me.
You hold a distorted view of what marriage means.
We have moved through life with a rhythm—
freely, spontaneously,
with organic synergy and silent accord.
But perhaps I shouldn't point that out either.
How many ways are we not already joined?
When have we asked much of each other,
yet given more than enough?

I do not want forever.
You misread what I may desire.
We are finite beings.
Why demand what no human can promise?
I wouldn't ask you for a fairytale—
just a lifetime.
But again, must I say this aloud?
You know me well enough to know—
I'm an enigma,
never ruled by convention.
Forever is for dreamers.
I live in the real.

Why would I crave anything beyond what we share—
a connection without excess language,
but full of presence and peace?
Still, I won't press the point.
You already know:
How we listen—
truly listen.
How we observe the quiet,
resolve the unspoken.

Why would I trade
this bond of minds,
this mutual respect,
this unconditional, quiet love—
for society's noise,
for roles, rituals, rules
designed to break hearts
and clutter minds?

Maybe some people
don't trust what is easy, real,
natural,
or good.

But I wouldn't dare point that out to you.

Closing Letter to the Reader

Dear Reader,

If you've made it here,
you already understand:
sometimes the deepest kind of love
is not the kind that pursues,
but the kind that waits—
still, unwavering, dignified.

This final poem was written after the letting go had begun,
but before the love had disappeared.
And that's the space *so many of us live in—*
between what was and what may never be again.
Not because we stopped loving,
but because someone else asked us for distance
we didn't want to give
but chose to honor anyway.

This isn't about surrendering power.
It's about honoring love without abandoning yourself.
It's about learning to hold on gently—
not to someone's body,
but to the *truth* of what you shared,
without suffocating either of you in the process.

I've written many things in these pages:
letters that reached for him,
poems that whispered through silence,
reflections wrapped in ache and restraint.
But this final piece—
this is the one that breathes.

Because here, I'm not begging.
I'm not chasing.
I'm not explaining.

I'm simply standing in love,
still and whole,
knowing that even in absence,
some connections remain untouched by time,
unchanged by distance.

If you've ever loved like this—
from a place of peace,
even in pain—
then I hope this book met you gently.

And if you're still in the silence,
still waiting,
still aching quietly in your own kind of space—
know that you are not alone.

This is not the end of the love.
Just the beginning of the becoming.

With stillness,
With strength,
With so much softness,

—Lueella Shelton

The Shape of Space

I have honored your plea—
the tender notice you gave
wrapped in ache and resignation.
I took your papers,
your silence,
and with shaking hands,
began to let the quiet speak
where once our words would bloom.

Last night, I messaged:
"I've made it home."
And as I pressed send,
grief rose like floodwater—
tears trapped in my throat,
my body trembling
at the thought
of no more good nights,
no more morning greetings
tied in text like ribbon on routine.

You taught me
to share my whereabouts,
to anchor you in the rhythm
of my coming and going.
That norm,
our norm,
now hangs like a question
between closed lips
and open wounds.

What does space look like
between two souls
who once moved
as one?

I will not chase you—
you asked for stillness
and I respect it.
But I will not
untether myself.
I will not release
the thread of us
unless your own hand
severs it first.

You sought me not—
I welcomed you.
And what a beautiful man I found.
A King.
A warrior.
A man of might,
measured not by bravado
but by the humility
of his gaze.

You will always be
exceptional in my eyes—
a man who can wear
his own crown
without apology.

Take your time.

Take all the time you need.

I'll wait here—
not moving on,
not reaching out,
but standing still
with a heart still calling your name
in the quiet
that now holds your absence.

Because space,
even space,
cannot erase
this love.
And I absolutely
adore you.
Still.
Forever.

Epilogue

The End of Us Was Never the End of Me

There is a particular kind of strength
in loving without losing yourself.
In staying soft
without staying stuck.

This book has been my offering—
to him, yes.
But also to the silence,
to the spaces that taught me how to listen
when love no longer spoke.

I wrote through the waiting.
I wrote through the ache.
And somewhere along the way,
I found a voice I hadn't heard in years—
my own.

This is where I leave the love unspoken.
Where I stop asking for answers.
Where I unclench my hands
and finally begin to gather
everything I gave away.

Not in bitterness.
Not in regret.
But in reverence for the woman
who chose to stay
until she was ready to rise.

Book Three: *Becoming Mine*
Letters from the Woman I Became

If this book held the silence,
the next one holds the return—
not of him,
but of me.

Becoming Mine is not a continuation of this love story.
It is the unfolding of a new one.
A story of healing.
Of identity.
Of coming home to the woman who was always there,
waiting to be chosen.

And this time—
she chooses herself.

I hope you'll meet me there.

With love still,
but no longer waiting,

—Lueella Shelton

About the Author

Lueella Shelton is a researcher, educator, and historian who writes with her whole heart and both hands open. Her work lives at the intersection of intimacy, identity, and emotional truth—offering readers an invitation to sit with longing, honor their own boundaries, and find beauty in the spaces between.

With a background in education and American history, Lueella weaves personal narrative with cultural memory, always centering the sacred in the everyday. Whether chronicling the ache of absence or the quiet strength of waiting, her poems are tender acts of witnessing—both of self and of love.

The Silence Between is the second in her trilogy, following her debut poetry collection, *The Spark and the Surrender*. While Book One captured the breathless beginnings—the want, the unfolding, the surrender—this volume dwells in the hush that follows. It is a record of letters never sent, questions never answered, and love that learns to speak louder than silence.

Lueella finds inspiration in late-night conversations, her handwritten letters, and the kind of love that leaves room for both closeness and solitude. She is a mother, a truth-teller, a keeper of stories, and a believer in the healing power of language.

When she is not writing, she is preserving history, mentoring young women, and sipping coffee strong enough to wake both body and spirit.

To follow her work, learn more, or connect, visit:

www.lulu-writes.com

Some stories don't end—they just grow quiet.

The Silence Between is the second book in Lueella Shelton's intimate trilogy—a raw, lyrical exploration of love, distance, and the ache of things left unsaid. These poems live in the hush that follows the spark, in the space between what was felt and what was never fully named.

Here, you'll find letters never sent, questions never answered, and moments that linger longer than they should. This is not a book of bitterness—it is a book of waiting, of witnessing, of learning how to love without losing your voice.

Written with unflinching tenderness, this volume is for anyone who has ever stayed too long in a love that could not stay with them. It is for the soft ones. The loyal ones. The ones who felt everything and still chose to speak with grace.

If Book One captured the spark, this is the quiet where longing echoes.

And when the silence has taught her all it can, she will rise.

Book Three: *Becoming Mine*
Letters from the Woman I Became

Coming soon.

www.ingramcontent.com/pod-product-compliance
Lightning Source LLC
Chambersburg PA
CBHW071200090426
42736CB00012B/2394